FRENCH
SEVENTEENTH CENTURY
PAINTING

FRENCH PAINTING

THE SEVENTEENTH CENTURY

by Margaretta Salinger
The Metropolitan Museum of Art

McGRAW-HILL BOOK COMPANY
New York   Toronto   London

FRENCH PAINTING

If one were asked to list quickly and informally the chief characteristics of the French seventeenth century a host of opposites would flock to mind: the splendor and extravagance of the court at Versailles and the austerity and sobriety of Jansenist religious ideas at Port Royal; the stupendous arrogance of Louis XIV, who equated the kingdom of France with his own individual person, and the touching simplicity and humility of the peasants painted by Louis Le Nain; the richness and variety of Le Brun's great decorations and the geometric severity of the deliberate and almost scientific compositions conceived by Poussin. A partial clue to the existence within a single century of this baffling array of violent contrasts is the fact that between 1600 and 1700 France was ruled by three successive monarchs, and it was only the reign of Louis XIV, from 1643 to 1715, the longest reign in French history, that is most aptly described as "splendid." This was the time of the greatest glitter, of the radiance that emanated directly from the person of the Sun King. French classicism, however, which was the unifying characteristic of the art, literature, and philosophy of the seventeenth century, flowered on ground tilled and prepared long before 1650.

The century opened with a decade of peace under Henri IV, who had established quiet relations between France and her neighbors and in 1598 had ended strife between Catholics and Protestants by issuing the famous Edict of Nantes, which assured the French Protestants, or Huguenots, freedom of conscience and freedom of worship. Henri IV made important improvements to the city of Paris which we still admire today: completing the Pont Neuf and laying out the Place Dauphine as well as the elegant and charming Place des Vosges. With the aid of his minister the Duc de Sully and a band of counselors that tolerantly included both Catholics and Protestants he pulled the country together, stabilizing finances, encouraging agriculture, renewing industry, and stimulating trade by building new roads, bridges, and canals.

In 1610 Henri IV was assassinated by a madman, and his second wife, Marie de' Medici, was made regent for their nine-year-old son Louis XIII. The affairs of France at home and abroad had worsened critically when in 1616 Armand Jean du Plessis, later Cardinal, de Richelieu (1585-1642) was named minister of state, charged with foreign affairs and war. A number of years were to pass, however, before he achieved his real power as First Minister of France. In 1617 the young king, with skillful backing and support — but more surprisingly with a sudden assertion of independence and will — took the reins of government into his own hands. He exterminated a crafty Italian couple, the Concini, who had exerted enormous and pernicious influence on his mother, and sent Marie herself into exile at Blois, where Richelieu followed her as chief counsellor. At the formal reconciliation of the king and the queen mother in the autumn of 1619, Richelieu too returned. Three years later the red hat, which had long since been promised, was bestowed on him, and in 1624 at the age of thirty-nine, having made himself indispensable, he was named chief minister.

Cardinal Richelieu was the youngest son of a nobleman and

only became a churchman because some member of the family was obligated to fill the family bishopric at Luçon in the west of France. It was really during his ministry and largely through his efforts that France made herself into one of the great powers of Europe. He lived to be only fifty-seven years old, but in less than two decades he accomplished the three purposes that he had avowed when he took office: the subduing of the Protestants, the humiliation of the arrogant and unruly nobility, and the elevation and glorification of the king's name. The wars that he instigated, the domestic reforms for which he was responsible, and the relative peace and prosperity that his judgment procured are a study in themselves, but it is important for an understanding of the seventeenth century and its art to acknowledge that it was Cardinal Richelieu who conceived the idea of absolute monarchy and gave it concrete form in his adroit championing of Louis XIII.

On the intellectual and artistic life of France he left permanent marks. It was he who founded the French Academy, the world's greatest monument to literature and semantics, and more than that, one of the great symbols of all time for intellectual standards and integrity. Like all powerful statesmen throughout history Richelieu was a builder. He entrusted his many grandiose schemes to the architect Jacques Lemercier (c. 1585-1654), who had spent about seven years studying in Rome. Before beginning to work for Richelieu, Lemercier had already been called on by the king to take part in the long process of enlarging and adding to the palace of the Louvre. The most important of Lemercier's buildings, and the largest number of them, however, were constructed at the order of the cardinal, who exacted of him not only several churches and châteaux, but even the design and the carrying out of an entire planned town on the site of the little village of Richelieu. Two of the most important buildings in Paris were built by Lemercier at the expense of Cardinal Richelieu; the Palais Cardinal and the Sor-

Figure 1.
François Girardon:
Tomb of Richelieu.
Sorbonne, Paris

bonne. The first, the large and sumptuous town residence of the chief minister, was made over by Richelieu shortly before his death as a gift to the Dauphin and then took its present name, Palais Royal. The Sorbonne, known throughout the world as one of the great centers of higher learning, was begun in 1626. The church of the Sorbonne, in which the cardinal is buried, was begun nine years later. The funerary monument in the church was made between 1675 and 1677 by the sculptor François Girardon (1628-1715), who had, like Lemercier, studied in Rome and was a close collaborator of the painter and master decorator Charles Le Brun. It shows the cardinal reclining on a chastely ornamented sarcophagus, supported in a sitting posture by an allegorical figure of Piety, and with a classically robed mourner at his feet (Figure 1).

Figure 2. Pierre Puget:
Milo of Crotona.
Louvre, Paris

Girardon, who supplied many statues for the gardens at Versailles and made an equestrian statue of Louis XIV which was in the Place Vendôme until it became a casualty of the French Revolution, displayed in all his work the classical style in which he had been trained during his years of study at the Academy. In contrast to him, his great contemporary and rival Antoine Coysevox (1640-1720) worked in a style much more inclined toward the Baroque. This French Baroque, however, unlike the Italian, is rather a question of compositional depth and diagonal movement than of sweeping and impassioned emotional disturbance.

The sculptor who may be regarded as the true shaper of French Baroque is Pierre Puget (1620-1694). A native of Marseilles, he spent three of his formative years working in Rome and Florence under Pietro da Cortona. Between 1659 and 1667 he was in Genoa, but spent most of the later part of his life in Toulon and Marseilles. In 1670 he found two blocks of marble in the dockyards at Toulon and from one of these fashioned his sculpture of *Milo of Crotona* (Figure 2). Milo was a Greek athlete of the archaic period, who, as an old man still confident from the feats of his youth, tried to break apart a split tree, which sprang back into a vise in which he was caught and devoured by wild beasts. Puget was never an artist of the French court, but his sculpture of Milo, which was placed in a prominent position in the gardens at Versailles, is a powerful work of art, revealing in the unity and thrust of its masses the strong impression made on the artist by the great Italian baroque sculptor Bernini.

The dying Richelieu himself recommended to Louis XIII his successor, Cardinal Mazarin, whom Richelieu had had named cardinal not long before. Mazarin (1602-1661) had been born in the Abruzzi of humble parentage, and his real name was Giulio Mazarini. He was well educated in Rome and in Spain and began his career as an officer in the army of the pope.

By 1630, however, he had made a name for himself as a diplomat and took the ecclesiastical habit. In 1634 he went as Papal Nuncio to the Court of Louis XIII, and there two years later left the service of the pope for that of the king of France, becoming a naturalized Frenchman in 1639. Louis XIII died in 1643, leaving a five-year-old son who became Louis XIV. Mazarin's charm facilitated his designs, and when Louis' widow, Anne of Austria, was designated regent, she made Mazarin her chief minister.

Mazarin's regime, which continued the policies instituted by Richelieu, was marked by the making of a famous peace and the waging of internal war in France. In 1648 the Treaty of Westphalia was signed at Münster, ending thirty years of political and religious carnage. But in the same year in France the civil war known as the *Fronde* broke out and for five years the embittered nobles warred against the crown. At its end in 1653 Mazarin returned to power for another eight years until his death.

He had amassed enormous wealth, which he spent, like Richelieu, upon building and great works of art. He became the owner of the old royal hunting lodge and château of Vincennes, redoing it and adding to it, and it was there that he died. He paid for the building of one wing of the still functioning hospice and mental hospital of the Salpêtrière in Paris. He bequeathed a huge sum of money for the founding of a college (Collège de Quatre Nations) for young men from the four provinces newly annexed to France by the Treaty of the Pyrenees. The gallery, adorned by the Italian artist Romanelli, was part of the complex of buildings known as the Palais Mazarin and today is part of the Bibliothèque Nationale, which houses the great treasure of books and manuscripts that he had collected. He had acquired from the impoverished banker Jabach some of his masterpieces of painting and these were in turn reacquired by Colbert for the state. Most important for the arts in France, it was

Cardinal Mazarin who founded in 1648 the Academy of Painting and Sculpture, which was carried on by Colbert and ultimately unified into a single Academy of Fine Arts in 1795.

Jean Baptiste Colbert (1619-1683) had been the administrator of Cardinal Mazarin's private fortune, knew his collections well, and in his time likewise became one of the great patrons and collectors of art in France. But during the last years of Mazarin's life control of all the revenues of France was in the hands of a powerful and unscrupulous man named Nicolas Foucquet. Immensely rich, Foucquet was the generous patron of the men of letters who flourished in France, including writers as famous as Molière and La Fontaine. At Mazarin's death in 1661 Foucquet had almost unlimited power, but the young king, advised by his expiring minister to take the government into his own hands and to dispense henceforth with chief ministers, began by listening to Colbert's exposure of Foucquet as an embezzler. Foucquet had indulged in a dazzling display of ostentation that angered Louis XIV by its boldness and prepared his mind for the undoing. He had planned a superb evening of entertainment for the king and court at Vaux-le-Vicomte, a sumptuous château built by the architect Louis Le Vau and surrounded by gardens designed by Le Nôtre (Figure 3). After

Figure 3.   Louis Le Vau:
Vaux-le-Vicomte.
Near Melun, France

9

Figure 4. Pierre Patel, the Elder: View of Versailles. Musée National, Versailles

supper the guests were diverted by a new comedy-ballet composed by Molière, with music by Lully and décor by Le Brun. Three weeks after this fabulous party Foucquet was disgraced and spent the rest of his life in the fortress of Pignerol. Colbert inherited his power, gained the confidence of the king, and took over Foucquet's army of artists and architects, who were henceforth employed in the royal buildings, especially the palace and gardens of Versailles, which owe much to the plans originated at Vaux-le-Vicomte.

In 1669 Le Vau transformed the old small château of Louis XIII at Versailles, giving it the new and splendid façade it has today (Figure 4). In the next decade huge wings were added

10

and the Galerie des Glaces installed by Jules Hardouin Mansart. He was the nephew of François Mansart, who had become famous for Maisons Laffitte, the reconstruction of Blois, and the plan and part of the building of Val-de-Grace, which the Queen Mother Anne of Austria had commissioned in fulfillment of a vow (Figure 5). Between 1671 and 1681 the Great Apartments of the king and queen at Versailles were decorated by Charles Le Brun (1619-1690). Le Brun, perhaps more than any other artist, had a profound influence on the arts of the seventeenth century in France, in his capacity as director of the Academy, director of the royal tapestry factory, and first painter to the king. He exercised a veritable dictatorship over the arts as long as Colbert lived, but at the minister's death he was supplanted by his rival Pierre Mignard. The Staircase of the Ambassadors and the splendidly decorated royal apartments, including the throne room dedicated to Apollo and the king's bedchamber in the center of the main axis of the palace, epitomize the "Grand Style of the Grand Epoch" in their symmetry, richness, and their invocation of classical mythology to do honor to Apollo's newest reincarnation, the Sun King, Louis XIV.

The recurrent theme that runs through all the biographies of French artists of the seventeenth century is whether or not they studied in Rome, and if not, how they received Italian influences through their more fortunate contemporaries. Indeed the attainment, or the denial, of the Prix de Rome remains through the eighteenth and nineteenth centuries one of the major preoccupations of painters. The two finest French painters of the splendid century, Poussin and Claude Lorrain, spent most of their working lives in Rome. Mignard worked there for twenty-two years. Others, like Vignon, Blanchard, and Vouet, spent some time there during the early years of their careers and then returned to work in France, their minds filled with Italian images and experiences which never, however, obliterated the strong native Frenchness that characterizes all the French art

Figure 5. François Mansart: Church of Val-de-Grâce. Paris

of the century. Still others received their knowledge of Italy indirectly: La Hire from Vouet, Blanchard and other returning painters and Le Sueur probably from engravings of the works of Raphael, which he easily could have known.

In Rome during the first years of the seventeenth century no artist made a louder claim to recognition than the notorious and revolutionary Michelangelo da Caravaggio (1573-1610), who changed the entire course of European painting. This genius, whose turbulent life came to an abrupt end when he was only thirty-seven, had his early training in Milan with a little-known painter from Bergamo. Before he was twenty he had migrated to Rome and had attracted the attention of numerous important patrons of art with realistic and freshly original paintings like the *Bacchus* of the Uffizi, *The Fortune Teller*, and the *Young Man Playing the Lute.* In 1590 he received the commission to paint three pictures of St. Matthew's life for the chapel of the deceased Cardinal Contarelli in the French church of Rome, San Luigi dei Francesi (Figure 6). The startling *Crucifixion of St. Peter* and *Conversion of St. Paul* in Sta. Maria del Popolo were painted in 1600-1601, after an intervening decade of prolific activity. Roman documents keep track of his stormy life as it lurched through quarrels and crimes, arrest and prison, until he died of a fever at Port'Ercole while making his way back from Naples to Rome to receive a papal pardon.

The most striking characteristic of Caravaggio's style was his use of sharp dramatic contrasts of light and dark. The pools of velvety black shadow were so much a trademark of his school that his followers, who were legion, fanning out into Spain, France, and the Netherlands, were often referred to as *tenebrosi* — the dark or shadowy ones. Abrupt movement, astonishing life-likeness, and strongly marked diagonals are other features of this artist's new and revolutionary way of painting (Figure 7).

Few of the painters who followed in Caravaggio's footsteps were more deeply impressed than the Frenchman Valentin de

Figure 6.
Michelangelo da Caravaggio:
Calling of Matthew.
San Luigi dei Francesi, Rome

Figure 7.
Michelangelo da Caravaggio:
Madonna of the Pilgrims.
St. Agostino, Rome

Boulogne (1591-1632). This young man, the son of a painter and stained-glass worker, had left his native town of Coulommiers in the Brie district in his early manhood, and had arrived in Rome before 1613. Our information about him comes from a few documents and the not altogether reliable testimony of the chronicler Sandrart. Patronage and fame came to him in the last few years of his life, when he worked for the important Cavaliere dal Pozzo and for Cardinal Barberini, the nephew of Pope Urban VIII, who had commissioned him to make an altarpiece for St. Peter's. Immediately after his death his paintings enjoyed an immense vogue, especially in France, where several were acquired by Cardinal Mazarin and five had the honor of hanging in the bedchamber of Louis XIV at Versailles. He handled large religious compositions and portraits with skill, but is best known for the half-length genre scenes in which he shows how deeply he assimilated the essentials of the style of Caravaggio. To this however he added a distinctly personal flavor which reveals itself best in the psychological penetration of human character and its expression in pose and mood (Color slide 1). Valentin, once seduced by Rome, never returned to his native land.

Another of the French artists who went to Rome in the years soon after Caravaggio's death was Claude Vignon (1593-1670), but Vignon, after a stay of about eight years, went back to France. Born in Tours, he had probably had some artistic education before leaving France, most likely in the late Mannerist style. He too fell deeply under the prevailing influence of Rome, but was introduced to it through the Northern disciples of Caravaggio, like Elsheimer and Lastman, the master of Rembrandt. In point of fact Vignon knew Rembrandt and sold some of his works in France. Vignon's style shows a mixture of his early training with what he had learned in Rome and his paint textures are distinguished by a rich impasto (Figure 8).

Two other French painters at work in Rome in the first

quarter of the seventeenth century were Jacques Blanchard (1600-1638) and Simon Vouet (1590-1649), but neither of them appears to have been deeply impressed by Caravaggism. Blanchard, like Vignon, had some training in the French Mannerist tradition, studying under his uncle Nicolas Bollery and later at Lyons with Horace Le Blanc. Arriving in Rome in 1624, he stayed about a year and a half before moving on to Venice, where the works of Titian and Veronese made a permanent impression upon him. He went back to Paris about 1628. Although Blanchard's style gives evidence of the strong Italian influence to which he submitted and also shows traces of the late works of Rubens, his color and his way of painting are not Italian, but French. In his decorative treatment of the nude especially, he always showed that the beginnings of his art were rooted in the tradition of the school of Fontainebleau (Color slide 2).

Simon Vouet (1590-1649) might be called the most influential of the French painters of the seventeenth century. It was his return to France in 1627 after fifteen years in Italy that made it possible for French stay-at-homes to know all the great Italian styles, since this precocious young artist traveled widely and absorbed into his own painting many different facets of Italian art. He is said to have gone to England as a boy of fourteen on a professional mission to paint a portrait and in 1611 to have journeyed to Constantinople with the French ambassador. From there, by way of Venice, he proceeded to Rome, which was his chief residence. In Rome he had the distinction, unusual for a young foreigner, of being elected president of the painters' guild, the Academy of St. Luke. Before returning home he seems to have visited many other Italian cities, including Genoa, Modena, and Bologna, and probably Naples.

Vouet's early style is imprinted with the influence of Caravaggio and reflections of Michelangelo's sculpture and shows too that he knew the painting of Lanfranco and Guercino. There is also in it, however, an element of the classic and academic, apparently drawn from familiarity with the work of Domenichino and Guido Reni. His subsequent decorative works in France reveal that he had profited during one or more visits to Venice by a careful examination of the decorations by Veronese. When Vouet returned to France he became almost immediately a successful artist, receiving numerous commissions to paint for private individuals and for churches. Some of his finest and most popular decorations were done in the chapel, the library, and the lower gallery of the Hôtel Séguier. Many important artists took their training with him, including Le Sueur, Pierre Mignard and his brother Nicolas, and Charles Le Brun himself, whose extensive influence spread Vouet's precepts into an even wider circle, and helped them to continue as the dominant ones throughout the century (Color slide 3).

Neither Eustache Le Sueur (1616-1655) nor his slightly older contemporary Laurent de La Hire (1606-1656) had the benefit of an on-the-spot experience with Italian art. The young Le Sueur became a pupil of Vouet, probably about 1632. His master's influence is clear in his earliest works, some designs for tapestries that Vouet had been asked to do himself but passed on to his young pupil. Later Le Sueur, working for the Hôtel Lambert, reveals along with Vouet's influence two new trends — the influence of Poussin and his classicism, and that of the High Renaissance painter Raphael, whose tremendous popularity is partly due to the widespread dissemination of engravings of his works (Color slide 4). Admiration for Raphael persisted with Le Sueur throughout his brief career, and in his last works we still find him borrowing motifs from Raphael's designs for tapestries.

Both Le Sueur and La Hire tempered their training and their reverence for the stronger personalities who shaped them with a subtle personal flavor born out of their own individuality and attitudes. In the case of Le Sueur, especially in his many religious works, the original component is a tone of reverence and withdrawn quietude. La Hire softened and flavored the classical style with his own lightness and subtle grace. He trained himself in France largely through making an attentive study of the great Fontainebleau decorations, which had been done by Italian artists and by Frenchmen working under the direction of the foreign visitors. It is thought too that he had seen some of the paintings by the great Venetians, which had been brought to Paris. Later the pervasive influences of both Poussin and Claude are easily traced in his work (Color slide 5).

In the east of France, at a considerable distance from Paris, the old independent duchy of Lorraine gave to French painting of the seventeenth century two of its most original and gifted figures, Claude Lorrain and the mysterious Georges de La Tour, who is probably the best exponent of French Caravaggism. Lorraine, at the beginning of the century, was far from being a provincial outpost, and two other important French artists were active there, Jacques Bellange and Jacques Callot. Little is known about Bellange except that between 1600 and 1617 he was recorded in Nancy, the capital of the duchy, as a painter of portraits and that for nine years, from 1602 until

Figure 9. Jacques Bellange: Orion Carrying Diana (Drawing). Private Collection

Figure 10.   Jacques Callot:
Temptation of St. Anthony.
National Museum, Stockholm

1611, he was in the service of Duke Charles III of Lorraine, painting murals and designing for theatrical performances. It is thought that he visited Rome before his activity in Nancy. Bellange's drawings and engravings reveal a highly original and graceful style in which two elements are combined — the small heads and extremities, the long proportions of the figures, the tossing drapery typical of Italian mannerism and the dexterous manual skill and exaggerated rhythms of late sixteenth-century engraving in the Low Countries (Figure 9). Jacques Callot (1592/93-1635), a native of Nancy, was an extremely prolific engraver, leaving behind him nearly fifteen hundred recorded etchings, as well as a great number of drawings (Figure 10).

Le Blond *excud.* auec Priuilege du Roy

Tandis que nos Maris s'on vont donner carriere / Et prendre leurs plaisirs a la ville ou au champs, / Mes Dames banquetons sus faisans chere entiere / N'espargnons rien non plus que font nos bons marchans.

Choisisse dans ces plats quel que morceau qui puisse / Vous mettre en apetit, s'esme le croupion, / De ce Coq d'inde froid pour vous leuer la cuisse / Beuuons mangeons icy n'est aucun espion.

Ie vous prie plus filer que premier, ie me mouille, / Fille versés du vin, ie vous veux beire d'autant. / La vin seroit meilleur si j'auois vne andouille, / Goustons de tous ces mets vous faut il prescher tant.

Fille a S.t Laurens vous aurez vostre faire: / Si vous ne dite mot de ce que nous faisons: / Ie ne sçaus si ie dois a vos promesse croire, / Ie ne sors du logis et garde les tisons.

.Bosse in et fe.

Figure 11.   Abraham Bosse: Wives at Table in the Absence of their Husbands (Engraving). Metropolitan Museum of Art, Dick Fund, 1926

He was apprenticed in Nancy to a goldsmith and engraver named Croce, but may have served under him only a short time, since sometime between 1608 and 1611 he went to Rome, where he studied with a French engraver. He worked for ten years in Florence for the Grand Duke Cosimo II, recording in his lively and perspicacious prints the ceremonies and festivities that took place at the Tuscan court. Returning to Nancy in 1621, he continued making etchings and won tremendous success. His more mature prints made at home in France exchanged for the mannered elegance and musical movement of his Florentine work a greater soberness, especially when he began to take his subject matter from sieges and battle scenes. During the twenties he worked in Brussels and in Paris, where Richelieu became his patron. His last great work is a series of etchings called the *Grandes Misères de la Guerre*, into which he poured a summary of the hideous events through which he and his contemporaries were living.

The greatest contrast to Callot's engravings is provided by those of another French contemporary printmaker, Abraham Bosse (1602-1676), to whom we are deeply indebted for pictures of the life led by comfortable well-to-do bourgeois, with accurate information about their homes, their furniture, their clothing, and their deportment (Figure 11). Bosse's clarity of composition and unfalteringly able technique are classically and quietly correct and perfectly adapted to the subject matter he depicted.

Vic-sur-Seille in Lorraine was the birthplace of Georges de La Tour (1593-1652), but most of his active and successful life was spent in Lunéville, not far from Nancy. He was a master there by 1620, operating a studio for training apprentice painters and fulfilling commissions. While he was still quite young the Duc de Lorraine ordered two works from him and later he is known to have been made King's Painter. In 1633 the Duchy of Lorraine was occupied by the French, who nearly destroyed the city of Lunéville, which is perhaps why La Tour was absent from there between 1639 and 1642. He returned however and spent the last decade of his life there. La Tour worked mostly for the bourgeoisie of Lorraine and for the French administrators who had their headquarters at Nancy.

Without any dependable evidence it has often been supposed that Georges de La Tour like so many of his countrymen had made the pilgrimage to Italy. The kind of naturalism and light and dark contrast that characterize his paintings, however, are less like the naturalism and chiaroscuro of Caravaggio himself, and more like these features as they appear when translated into the idiom of Caravaggio's Dutch followers, such as Terbrugghen. Scholars have therefore presumed that La Tour made one or even two journeys to the Low Countries. In any case the style that he finally evolved, whatever influences contributed to its development, is beautiful and definitively his own (Color slides 6, 7, 8). In many of his paintings the mood is established by the use of candle-lighting. This artificial form of illumination gives to the quiet huddled groups an air of hushed solemnity and secrecy, as if their meetings were deliberately clandestine, like those of the early Christians in the catacombs. Members of the Holy Family at work or in meditation, or saints in remote self-communion or ecstasy have never been given more poignant and moving images than in the works of Georges de La Tour.

The humble people painted by Louis Le Nain, the best and finest of the three brothers Le Nain, are not, like those of Georges de La Tour, characters from a sacred story, but usually peasants, represented with exquisite tenderness, but without a trace of sentimentality. Pieter Bruegel and Vincent van Gogh liked to paint peasants, but both of these artists managed always to make them clumsy and ugly peasants, twisted and beaten by life's abuses into gracelessness. Millet and Dagnan-Bouveret in the nineteenth century also had a predilection for the working people of the village and the farm, but always with the false implication that there is necessarily something ennobling and beautiful about poverty and hard work. There is always beauty and dignity and serenity in the figures of Louis Le Nain.

The three brothers Le Nain and the attribution of their paintings remain a difficult problem because they sometimes seem to have collaborated on the same work, and the small group of signed and dated pictures bear only the signature "Le Nain." Antoine (ca. 1588-1648), Louis (1593-1648), and Mathieu (1607-1677) Le Nain were all born in Laon. Antoine, who is said to have "excelled in miniatures and portraits in

small," had transferred to Paris by 1629. There he became master painter to the Abbey of St. Germain des Prés. The paintings that are thought to be by him are for the most part small, on copper, and often represent bourgeois families. They are in a style that shows Antoine must have been strongly influenced by Dutch painters such as Avercamp. Louis, the best painter of the three, had turned up in Paris, still an apprentice, by 1630. It has been suggested that he made the customary painter's trip to Rome, and he is said to have been an imitator of the Dutchman Pieter van Laer, called Bamboccio, whom he could have known in Italy or when that painter of humorous genre scenes passed through France. Louis' style, however, is solemn and moving rather than comical. His very refined range of low-keyed color, the firmness and dignity of his figures, and the serenely poetic landscapes that often form his settings combine to produce paintings of classical spirit and very high quality (Color slides 9, 10).

Mathieu Le Nain, the youngest of the three, practiced his craft for nearly three decades after his brothers had died. His success came earlier than theirs, for at the age of twenty-seven he was master painter to the city of Paris. Although the influence of Louis can be traced in his work, worldliness and sophistication characterize his paintings just as they characterize the recorded facts about his life. He appears to have achieved wealth and honor, becoming a knight, a lieutenant in the city militia, and the owner of a farm, and he was buried in state from the Parisian church of St. Sulpice. His pictures are typically genre scenes of well-dressed upper-class young men, amusing themselves with wine or card games as in Dutch pictures of officers taking recreation (Color slide 11).

The sobriety and unadorned impressive strength of Louis Le Nain's peasant scenes are related to a phenomenon widely observable in French intellectual and spiritual life in the seventeenth century. The prevailing attitude of the century was serious or religious. It was not only the age that produced the philosopher Descartes and the saints François de Sales and Vincent de Paul. It was perhaps the only period in history when "sacred eloquence," or preaching, was so important and of such high quality that it could be listed among the arts. Among the famous preachers were Jacques Bossuet, François Fénelon, and Louis Bourdaloue, whose sermons even the critical and questioning Mme. de Sévigné loved to hear.

In such a climate it is not surprising to encounter an enthusiastic and devoted cult of Jansenism, or the revival of the doctrines of St. Augustine and their adaptation to the spiritual needs of the seventeenth century. Named for the Dutch theologian Cornelius Jansen (1585-1638), this movement was centered in France in the old Cistercian abbey of Port Royal, a few miles southwest of Paris, near Marly. There the nuns, under the spell of the energetic Angélique Arnauld, came in contact with Jansen's friend and chief French apostle, Jean Duvergier, and put into practice the austere and unspectacular form of Christianity that was extolled by Jansen and opposed to the practices of the Jesuits. For more than half a century, condemned by two popes and in 1660 by Louis XIV himself, the convent and the school run by the "hermits," or semi-monastic laymen, followed with devotion and reforming zeal their exigent faith. In 1709 the last nuns were forcibly removed and the property was given to the College of St. Cyr. The classic dramatist Jean Baptiste Racine was educated in the school of Port Royal, and Blaise Pascal, retiring to its hermitage, wrote the famous philosophic letters, the *Provinciales,* which defended the Jansenists against the Jesuits, and also the fragments of a great projected treatise, published as the *Pensées.*

Philippe de Champaigne (1602-1674) (a Flemish artist by birth who became in France the special painter of Cardinal Richelieu) through the sadness of his personal life was deeply affected by Jansenism, which he embraced. Born in Brussels, he studied with minor Flemish painters before going at the age of nineteen to France, where he worked under Georges Lallemand and took part in the decorating of the Luxembourg Palace. He was established as an important painter in Paris before he reached his thirtieth birthday. Although he was famous for his portraits, his acceptance of Jansenism gave to his religious paintings a calm and classical quality which sets them aside as impressive contributions to French art (Color slide 12). He had a daughter who was a nun at Port Royal, where she was miraculously cured of an illness from which she had suffered since childhood. His votive picture commemorating this event includes no baroque manifestations of divine intervention, but simply the sick young woman on a chaise-longue and beside her the kneeling figure of the pious abbess whose special prayers helped to bring about the cure.

Another painter whose religious pictures are distinguished by the peculiar sobriety of the seventeenth century is Jean Tassel (c. 1608-1667). Like his father Richard, with whom he was for many years confused, he received much of his artistic education in Italy. In 1634 he was in Rome, where he admired Raphael, the followers of Caravaggio, and Guido Reni. He also visited Venice and saw the works of Veronese. Back home in France, he worked in Langres (the town from which his family came), as well as in Troyes and Dijon, affirming his essential Frenchness by rejecting drama for the sake of expressing character and atmosphere. The studied simplicity of such a portrait as Tassel's nun (Color slide 13), indeed all the spiritual discipline of Port Royal finds a parallel in the ideology of Nicholas Poussin.

Poussin (1593/94-1665) was surely the greatest artist of the French seventeenth century and the most typical, expressing — through a rigid series of principles which he applied to the structure of his paintings — the entire moral and intellectual temper of his age in France. Although he spent all but two of his productive years in Rome, the great body of works that he did in Italy is uniformly and overwhelmingly French. Poussin was born near Les Andelys in Normandy, the son of a poor man, who cannot, however, be labeled a peasant. He left home in 1612 to become a painter, going first to Rouen, where he took some lessons from Noël Jouvenet. Before the year was out we find him in Paris, where he probably studied under Lallemand. Even more important than formal lessons in painting were the opportunities that Paris offered a gifted young provincial to study in the Royal Library and the royal collections of painting and sculpture. Here Poussin must have taken an early interest in the Roman statues and reliefs, in the engravings after Raphael, and most of all in the paintings by Raphael and Titian preserved there. During his stay in Paris he worked with Philippe de Champaigne on the decorations of the Luxembourg Palace.

In 1624 he arrived in Italy, where he worked in the studio of Domenichino for a time. He was poor, but through a chain of introductions from his Paris days he came to the attention of Cardinal Francesco Barberini, the nephew of Pope Urban VIII. Through him Poussin received a commission to paint a large altarpiece for St. Peter's. It was the cardinal's secretary Cassiano del Pozzo, however, who became one of his most understanding patrons, when, toward the end of the thirties, Poussin stopped trying to paint large imposing pictures which reflected the various Italian stimuli to which he responded (Color slide 14) and began to produce small poetic interpretations of classical mythology and Tasso. These pictures are very reminiscent of Titian. By the end of the thirties these gentle elegiac pictures had given way to carefully planned and balanced paintings,

Figure 13. Nicolas Poussin: Ordination of St. Peter (Drawing). Pierpont Morgan Library, New York

27

which substitute for the lyrical charms of color and landscape stable poses and the deliberate conveying of various emotions through gesture and facial expression.

In 1640 Poussin's serious pursuit of his art according to moral and aesthetic principles and his careful study of all the visible remnants of Roman antiquity was interrupted by an unhappy period of a little more than a year and a half in Paris, in obedience to the summons of Louis XIII and Cardinal Richelieu. Unalluring commissions for grandiose pictures and designs for decorating the Louvre combined with the jealous intrigues of the Parisian artists to send him eagerly back to Rome, which he never left again. The only blessing of the Paris sojourn was a series of new contacts and friendships, especially with Paul Fréart de Chantelou for whom he painted a self-portrait (Color slide 17).

Between his return to Rome and his death twenty-three years later, Poussin's works divide into two groups. The first of these includes the paintings in the original style for which he is chiefly known and which proved to be one of the strongest influences on French painting all the way down to Cézanne. He treated the great Christian themes and subjects drawn from the social historians, rigorously striving for clarity and unity and working, as Anthony Blunt so well phrased it, toward the "mathematically rational principles which governed Descartes' view of the material world." Landscapes of great beauty formed the background for some of these paintings; yet they were not treated for their power to express mood or poetry, but like the figures were manipulated into the over-all scheme (Color slides 15, 16).

Poussin achieved the stylistic effects that have become inextricably commingled in our minds with the entire concept of "classicism" through an orderly and thorough working method. His preparation to paint a picture included an exhaustive reading about his subject, the fashioning of wax figures, first small ones, then large, to be draped and moved about on a model stage, and the making of a great many sketches. He never painted directly from life.

In his last years he painted some of his most glorious pictures, abandoning specific themes for more generalized allegories of man and nature. If these lofty late pictures are somewhat difficult to understand, it is because their appeal is directed to the mind and not to the senses. This is the essence of the raging controversy historically known as the opposition between the "Poussinistes" or followers of Poussin's often chill ideals and the "Rubenistes", who embraced rather the sensuous style of the great Flemish painter.

In the strict doctrinaire teaching of the French Academy, Poussin, along with the ancients and Raphael, was set before young students of painting as a prescribed example. His use of noble subject matter and his dedication to the principle that reason should prevail over the senses in the making of a work of art were exactly paralleled in the precepts of the Academy's formal lectures. Pierre Mignard, who replaced Le Brun as director of the Academy in 1690, had been trained by Vouet. He had spent about twenty years in Italy, chiefly in Rome, when in 1657 Louis XIV summoned him back to Paris. There he quickly became successful painting decorations, but chiefly as a portraitist (Color slide 18).

Two other painters whose fame rests chiefly on their portraits are Hyacinthe Rigaud (1659-1743) and Nicolas de Largillière (1656-1746). Although their life spans stretch well into the middle of the eighteenth century, they form a transition from the period of Louis XIV and, like most transitional figures, point up with clarity the character of the age from which they evolved. Rigaud came from Perpignan, near the Spanish border. His first provincial masters introduced him to the style of the Flemish painter Van Dyck, so that he already had a disposition toward great portrait painting when he reached the Royal

Academy in Paris and was urged by Le Brun to exchange historical painting for the field of portraiture. He had already painted the king's brother and the regent and received numerous commissions from the court, the aristocracy and the church when in 1694 he painted his first portrait of Louis XIV. He has been called the "born painter of kings," since five monarchs sat to him and four generations of the French royal family. His formula for state portraits includes a rich Flemish use of color, and the elegance with which he clothes his subjects has a breezy baroque quality and a strong tendency toward rococo grace (Color slide 19).

Although born in Paris, Largillière got his training from Flemish painters, studying under Antoine Goubeau in Antwerp where he became a member of the painter's guild. Later, in London, he worked as an assistant to Pieter Lely. In 1682 he went back to Paris, became a member of the French Academy, and launched a successful career as a painter of portraits of the rich middle-class (Color slide 20). He also created a picture (now unfortunately destroyed) of the municipal magistrates of Paris seated at a table, a French parallel to the group portrait so important in seventeenth-century Dutch painting, made especially famous by Rembrandt and Hals. The work assigned to Largillière when he was employed in London by Pieter Lely consisted in providing drapery and still life for Lely's pictures. This he was no doubt well prepared to do, since his youthful master Goubeau was known as a painter of still life. As a new member of the Academy, Largillière probably was somewhat ashamed of his humble beginnings, for the painting of still life was not according to the Academy a highly respected branch of the painter's art. Nevertheless, in seventeenth-century France, just as in the Low Countries, this very appealing kind of picture developed into an important aspect of independent painting.

Probably the finest of the French still-life painters of the beginning of the century is the mysterious artist Baugin, of whom little is known except the internal evidence provided by three extremely fine pictures (Color slide 21). Two of them are signed simply with the surname "Baugin"; the third is signed "A. Baugin" and bears an inscription stating that the artist was working in Paris in 1630 and that this is the year in which the picture was painted. The still-life specialist Charles Sterling thinks Baugin probably made the customary journey to Rome and combined what he saw there of Caravaggio with his native Northern tendencies. He points out the geometrical rigor and rationalism of his arrangement.

A painter from Strasbourg named Sébastien Stoskopff (1595-1657) worked at about the same time as Baugin and in his linear clarity and precision bears him a certain amount of resemblance (Figure 14). Stoskopff spent over twenty years in Paris, but returned in 1641 to Strasbourg and stayed there until the end of his life. The still-life paintings by Jean-Baptiste

Figure 14.
Sébastien Stoskopff:
Still Life. Strasbourg Museum

31

Monnoyer (1636-1699) and Alexander François Desportes (1661-1743), in contrast to the spare and discriminatingly selective ones by Baugin and Stoskopff, are opulent and billowing (Color slide 22). Both Monnoyer and Desportes were solidly grounded in the Flemish tradition. Monnoyer began his studies in Antwerp before establishing himself with great success in Paris. Through Le Brun he participated in the great decorative schemes for adorning domestic architecture, and something by him was in most of the residences of Louis XIV. On the invitation of an English lord he went to London, and spent the last two decades of his life working for Queen Anne and the owners of palatial English country houses. Desportes began by painting portraits and worked at that for a year at the Polish court. Later in France he contributed, like Monnoyer, to the adornment of the royal châteaux, made tapestry cartoons, and painted still lifes filled with precious objects (Figure 15). Among his other talents Desportes had a gift for landscape, making sketches directly from nature, which he used as backgrounds for hunting scenes.

It was a landscapist who took the place of preeminence second only to Poussin. Claude Lorrain (1600-1682), whose real name was Gellée, came from a village near Nancy in Lorraine and as a boy learned the trade of pastry cook. When still very young he went to Rome, not to study painting, but to practice this modest but respectable *métier*. It happened, however, that the work he found was in the house of a landscape painter, Agostino Tassi, where he abandoned *pâtisserie* for painting. He left Rome to visit Naples and returned to Nancy for a couple of years before settling in Rome in 1627, where he remained for the rest of his life.

Beside his master Tassi, the painters from whom Claude took his notion of the elements of classical landscape were Paul Bril and Adam Elsheimer, and at first his pictures resembled theirs in sharp and dramatic contrasts of light and shadow. His

Figure 15.
François Desportes: Still
Life. Musée de Lyons

landscapes soon evolved in grandeur and in an original concep-
tion of lofty views and distances, in an artistic development
that paralleled his rapidly increasing fame (Color slides 23,
24). He came to know Poussin and with him made sketching
trips in the Roman countryside. Like Poussin he studied space
and gave great attention to arranging and composing it in a way
that most impressively ennobled his finished paintings. His pictures often have classical or mythological subjects, but the figures in them, as in the purer landscapes where the peasants are

part of the pastoral scheme, are small in relation to the towering mountains and trees and the endless rippling sea (Figure 16). It has been said that Claude's greatest early innovation was his painting of the sun, and that through it he gave unity to his pictures. Like Claude Monet, the great French Impressionist who worked with the same intention two centuries later, Claude Lorrain studied with patience and devotion the delicate nuances of light at different seasons and at different times, and his pictures, like Monet's, record particular effects of light. There is a certain value in ending a study of French painting of the seventeenth century with the name of Claude Lorrain, for it proves that along with the widely divergent qualities of splendor, realism, moral discipline and rationalism, this age had room as well for reverence toward nature.

Figure 16. Claude Lorrain: Landscape with Cattle (Drawing). The Cleveland Museum of Art, Gift of Mr. and Mrs. Edward B. Greene

COMMENTARY ON THE COLOR SLIDES

· 1 ·

VALENTIN
DE BOULOGNE
(1591–1632)

The Concert

Oil on canvas,
67⅜″ x 83½″
Louvre, Paris

This picture passed through very famous hands before it came into the possession of the Louvre, having once belonged to Louis XV. It is one of a pair of closely similar paintings by Valentin in the Louvre, which are both good and typical examples of the kind of subject for which this artist was famous.

The plumed ornately dressed performer at the right, with his brocaded sleeve and his long sword at his side, recalls figures in works by Caravaggio. A contrived but satisfactory balance is achieved by the closely knit group at the extreme left, which is made up of a wistful and poetic youth who bows his head over the bass viol he is playing and a musician in armor, seen from the back. Many of the faces bear a strong resemblance to each other in shape and expression, and this unity of appearance is strengthened by the fitful play of chiaroscuro that moves in bright patches and dark velvety shadows across the canvas.

It is characteristic of Valentin's work that even in a rowdy scene of low life and insistent noise, an element of melancholy and deep feeling establishes a haunting and unforgettable mood.

· 2 ·

JACQUES BLANCHARD
(1600–1638)

Angelica and Medor

Oil on canvas,
47⅞″ x 69¼″
Metropolitan Museum of Art,
New York. Gift of
George A. Hearn, 1906

The subject of this painting is taken from *Orlando Furioso*, a long poem by the famous Italian author Ariosto. In Canto XIX he records how the lovers Angelica and Medor carved each other's names on the bark of an oak tree. A good copy of the picture in England has an inscription on the trunk of the tree, showing the first letters of the name Medor. Although this proof that the subject has been correctly identified has disappeared from the Metropolitan Museum's picture, it must have been there originally, just as it appears in the copy.

Not only the subject matter, but the style in which the picture is painted has its origin in Italy, where Blanchard went as a young man to study art in Venice and Rome. The rich foliage of the deeply shadowed grove where the lovers sit, the poetic glimpse of sky, paling at the horizon, and the idealized figures — his semi-draped and hers nude — strongly recall great pictures painted by Titian and Tintoretto at the high point of the Italian Renaissance. Félibien, a critic who was a contemporary of Blanchard but outlived him by many years, observed that "he much enjoyed painting naked women" and that he had so much facility "that he is known to have painted an entire figure, life-size, in two or three hours."

· 3 ·

SIMON VOUET
(1590–1649)

*Saint Charles Borromeo Prays
for the Plague-Stricken*

Oil on canvas, 137¾" x 98¼"
Musée des Beaux Arts,
Brussels

Saint Charles Borromeo, "the good saint," and indeed one of the most popular saints of the Counter-Reformation, had been dead less than three decades when Vouet went to Italy in 1612. A member of an old and wealthy family and nephew of Pope Pius IV, Charles was created Cardinal and Archbishop of Milan at the youthful age of twenty-three and lived for three years in Rome at the court of his uncle the Pope before taking up his duties in Milan. In the Milan See he devoted himself to ecclesiastical reform and widespread works of charity and social improvement. Most of the famous Italian baroque artists painted scenes from his life or included him in representations of groups of saints. All of them, and Vouet too, seem to have been guided by some authentic portrait made while he lived, showing him with a thin beardless face, a large mouth, and the noticeably sharp and bony aquiline nose that distinguishes him in our picture. The scene taking place occurred during the outbreak of the plague in Milan in 1575. While everyone who could was flying from the city, St. Charles calmly and deliberately went about, helping the sick, preaching and administering the Sacrament, and burying the dead. Finally, after walking barefoot through the city, he prostrated himself before the crucifix in the Cathedral, as we see him here, offering his own life as a sacrifice and plea for the cessation of the plague. Christ and the Virgin appear in answer to his prayer and an angel may be seen sheathing the sword of God's wrath.

Vouet probably painted this picture around 1640. The massive order and regularity of the architecture and its contrast of verticals and horizontals in the columns and the brightly lit steps of the altar, organize the baroque elements of the picture's composition into a characteristically French painting of the seventeenth century.

· 4 ·

EUSTACHE LE SUEUR
(1617–1655)
The Death of St. Bruno
Oil on canvas, 76″ x 51⅛″
Louvre, Paris

This scene of the death of St. Bruno, surrounded by the white-robed brothers of his order of Carthusians, is generally regarded as the best of the twenty-two pictures dedicated to this saint that were painted by Le Sueur between 1645 and 1650. The series was made for the great Carthusian monastery of Paris, in the Rue d'Enfer. At the beginning of the nineteenth century the paintings were displayed at Versailles and subsequently in the Luxembourg Palace, before entering the Louvre in 1818.

St. Bruno, who became a favorite saint of the Counter-Reformation, lived in the eleventh century. He was a scholar and teacher who had come from Cologne. After experiencing a frightening miracle he founded the very strict order of Carthusians in 1084. The first house of the order was near Grenoble in France in the town of Chartreuse, from which the monks took their name. Their severe rule stressed fasting, silence, and the suppression of almost all physical comforts. Carthusians, following their scholarly founder, became famous for their fine libraries, and in their monasteries great numbers of books were transcribed and preserved. They were also distinguished as horticulturists, the finest in Europe, and were famous for their skill in gardening. St. Bruno died at a Carthusian monastery in Calabria in 1101, and his relics were found four centuries later. He was cannonized in 1623.

When Le Sueur was commissioned to paint his series of scenes from the life and death of the saint, many other artists of Italy and Spain had already made suites of such paintings. The most famous were by Crespi, Guercino, and Stanzione. Ribalta and Zurbarán in Spain dedicated pictures to the subject of St. Bruno, and there was a cycle of fifty-six by Carducho, with which Le Sueur certainly seems to have been familiar.

· 5 ·

LAURENT DE LA HIRE
(1606–1656)

*The Children of Bethel
Mourned by their Mothers*

Oil on canvas, 38⅛″ x 50¾″
Signed and dated:
L. de la Hyre in. et F. 1653.
Musée du Palais Saint-Vaast,
Arras

This painting, like a number of other pictures that La Hire painted toward the end of his life, shows very clearly the influence of Claude Lorrain, in the treatment of the ruined classical temple and especially in the lyrical character of the landscape and the golden light that floods it. At the beginning of his career, up to about 1640, La Hire's works, under the influence of the Italian baroque artists, especially Caravaggio, had showed strong movement and great contrasts of light and dark, producing violent effects. This period was succeeded, however, by a classical decade in which his painting was strongly reminiscent of Poussin.

The sorrowful but tranquil scene depicted here, the grief of the classically robed mothers over their dead children takes its subject from a shockingly vengeful story of the Old Testament. In the second chapter of the second *Book of Kings* it is related how the prophet Elisha, going up from Jericho to Bethel, was taunted by a group of children. He cursed the children — an event that modern readers might perhaps attempt to explain by the fact that he was no doubt shaken by recent experiences he had had, including witnessing the miracle of his master Elijah's ascent into Heaven in a fiery chariot and his own inheritance of the prophet's mantle. At his curse, two she-bears appeared from the woods and tore to pieces forty-two of the children.

· 6 ·

GEORGES DE LA TOUR
(1593–1652)

The Adoration of the Shepherds

Oil on canvas, 42⅛″ x 54″
Louvre, Paris

There is good reason for believing that this is the picture ordered from La Tour in 1644 by the municipal councilors or aldermen of Lunéville as a gift for the governor of Nancy. It is recorded that the artist received seven hundred francs, a comparatively high price. In a circular composition beloved by La Tour, five figures — the Virgin, St. Joseph, two shepherds, and a woman who is perhaps St. Anne — encircle the basket of straw on which the Christ Child in His swaddling clothes lies sleeping. St. Joseph holds a large brightly-burning candle in his right hand, shielding it with his left, the fingers illuminated in a way that may be seen in a number of other pictures by the same artist. The figures are physically united in the glow of this candle, just as they are made spiritually one in their loving worship of the little child. The model who posed for the quiet serenely beautiful figure of the Virgin Mary was used again in another picture, where she represents St. Anne. The young shepherd with a staff and a lamb reminds us vividly of types often seen in pictures by Louis Le Nain.

GEORGES DE LA TOUR
(1593–1652)

*Saint Mary Magdalen
with a Candle*

Oil on canvas, 50½″ x 37″
Louvre, Paris

St. Mary Magdalen is honored in the Gospels as one of the greatest examples of true and full repentance, whose sins were all forgiven by Jesus. The Golden Legend records how after the Crucifixion, she went by boat with her brother Lazarus and her sister Martha to France, where they preached the Gospel and converted heathens, first in Marseilles and then in Aix, and how after thirty years of solitary repentance in the desert she died. Her relics are enshrined in the abbey church at Vézelay. The Magdalen was a popular saint in the seventeenth century and apparently a favorite with Georges de La Tour, who painted at least three pictures of her and named one of his daughters after her.

This solitary penitent, meditating at night in deepest solitude, was a subject of the kind he liked best to paint. The emphasis he laid on the conical flame, which is the sole source of the picture's light, reminds us how the Golden Legend called the saint herself a "light." The scene presents a pure distillation of deep, but almost unemotional, reflection and sorrow. The device of fixing the Magdalen's gaze not on the skull itself, but on the pure base of the flame, carries her a step beyond the immediate experience of thinking and feeling into an abstract realm of memory and resignation. The exquisitely sensuous touch of the slender fingers that rest so delicately on the skull seems to convey their melancholy message in an undertone. The Magdalen is the patron saint of the gypsies, and La Tour has given her fine sharp profile and the curving mass of her black hair the same gypsy look that he gave to the thieving girls in *The Fortune Teller*.

· 8 ·

GEORGES DE LA TOUR
(1593–1652)

The Fortune Teller

Oil on canvas, 40⅛″ x 48⅝″
Metropolitan Museum of Art,
New York. Purchase,
Rogers Fund, 1960

Fortune telling and cheating at cards — another subject La Tour painted — were popular seventeenth-century genre themes made famous by examples invented in Italy by Caravaggio and repeated by his admirers and imitators all over Europe. The aristocratic but naively inexperienced young man in this picture, who has sometimes been wrongly identified as the Prodigal Son, is shown surrounded by gypsies engaged in relieving him of his valuables while his attention is concentrated on an old crone who holds out to him a coin or medal. He stands enclosed in a half-circle formed by the four women. The young one at the left slips his purse from his pocket and is about to place it in the open hand of her dusky-haired sister close beside her, while a young and innocent-looking girl with a smooth, brilliantly lighted porcelain-like face turns on him a sidelong gaze as her busy hands deftly snip his gold medal from the end of a long chain he wears across his shoulder. It is hard to tell whether the wrinkled old woman is reciting an incantation, as one scholar has suggested, that might determine, rather than predict, the future or whether she is trying to sell him something, which we may be sure is worthless.

La Tour probably painted this picture very early in his career, perhaps before 1633. It is one of a small group of pictures unusual in his work, which are daylight, rather than night scenes. This one is also unusual in its bright variety of color and its full rich decorative detail. Only the young hero is dressed in a costume that has no pattern except on the border of his collar, and this plainness of surface helps the artist to isolate him from the garish circle of thieves into which he has stumbled. In the women's costumes there is great variety in the headdresses and the garments and the artist has ranged with virtuosity from the subtle painting of the guimpe of the young blonde to the brilliance of the embroidered glitter on the sleeve at the left and the glowing splendor of the old woman's patches of oriental brocade.

· 9 ·

LOUIS LE NAIN
(1593–1648)

The Peasants' Meal

Oil on canvas, 38⅛″ x 48″
Signed and dated:
Le Nain fecit ano 1642.
Louvre, Paris

In the last century, before this picture was acquired by the Louvre, it had a title which illuminates its subject matter, *Le Fermier bienfaisant,* or The Beneficent Tenant-Farmer. A small jug of red wine and a little crusty loaf, which are the only edibles visible, surely do not constitute a meal, and there seems to be a clear and intentional distinction between the refined and sensitive man in the middle and the coarsely dressed peasants at either side of him. A youth with a fiddle provides a musical accompaniment, while a woman, two small boys, and a dog are unparticipating witnesses to the scene. The setting is not a peasant's hut, but a fairly lofty room, with a shuttered window, a huge fireplace, and a structure in the background at the right which is probably a curtained bed, built into the wall. The dignity and seriousness of the figures and the mood of solemn gravity that is so characteristic of Louis Le Nain's paintings of peasants leads us to go one step farther and see not a picture of a gentleman treating two of his employees to a glass of wine, but a very unusual and moving treatment of the biblical subject of the Supper at Emmaus. This was the mystical moment when the resurrected Christ, supping with two of his saddened and forlorn followers in a country inn, blessed bread and wine, revealing suddenly in that act his true identity. A glow of light from the fire behind the head of the central figure suggests a halo, which strengthens this interpretation.

· 10 ·

LOUIS LE NAIN
(1593–1648)

Peasants in a Landscape

Oil on canvas, 16¼″ x 21¾″
Wadsworth Atheneum, Hartford.
The Ella Gallup Sumner and
Mary Catlin Sumner Collection

No other work by Louis Le Nain or his brothers has so much right to be regarded as a pure landscape, and yet this view differs from other landscapes by seventeenth-century painters in being a completely humanized outdoor scene. It is not only the group of quiet reposeful figures in the foreground, including the curled-up dog, which sets the mood of country peace and wholesomeness. In the middle ground, near the little Gothic chapel, a girl balancing a large crock on her head follows a grazing cow, a young shepherd with a crook watches over a flock of nibbling sheep, and at the left a lady with a little child greets a gentleman whose cavalier costume, even at a considerable distance, labels him the lord of this or a neighboring manor. The towers built in the architectural style of Louis XIII rise in a walled enclosure at the left, and at the far right, silhouetted against the bright horizon of a cloud-streaked sky, are the roofs of a village.

The two chief foreground figures are heavy and still, their broad and weighted shapes echoed and emphasized by the assemblage of homely objects that surround them — the dilapidated wooden barrel, the wicker basket, the crockery, and even the stool and the rocks. They listen to the piping of a young shepherd in a white blouse seated at a little distance back, and one deduces especially from the careworn face of the woman who gazes out at the spectator that this serene moment of rest is only a brief respite in a life of unremitting care and work.

· 11 ·

MATHIEU LE NAIN
(1607–1677)

The Tricktrack Players

Oil on canvas, 35⅜" x 47¼"

Louvre, Paris

Tricktrack is a kind of backgammon and the young men engaged in playing it, like the young fellow looking on from behind the table, evidently belong to the well-to-do, if not aristocratic, upper classes. Their clothes are stylish and their postures casual and self-confident. Mathieu Le Nain himself, who was known as the Chevalier Le Nain, was a lieutenant of the king's bourgeois company and spent much time in military circles and high society in Paris, where he must have known many young cavaliers like the ones in this picture. The two more plainly dressed and sober young boys at either side of the players act as foils and contrasts and are probably valets. Many similar scenes were being painted in Holland about the same time, but this one differs from them in the almost complete absence of circumstantial description of the room. Dutch genre paintings usually establish exactly the architecture and furniture of the apartments in which the scenes take place; here only the heavy oriental tablecloth with its rich pattern is given emphasis and the plain walls and floors have only subtle gradations of light and tone and strong cast shadows to lend them decorative interest.

Mathieu, who was trained by his older brothers, especially Louis, lived on twenty-nine years after they had died and in his later painting was influenced by the work of the Dutch "little masters."

· 12 ·

PHILIPPE DE
CHAMPAIGNE
(1602–1674)

Portrait of Cardinal Richelieu

Oil on canvas, 87⅞" x 61"

Louvre, Paris

This imposing portrait of Louis XIII's prime minister, dressed in his cardinal's robes and wearing around his neck the cross of the Order of the Holy Ghost, is one of several that Philippe de Champaigne painted between 1635 and 1640. In the pose and the effect of majestic elegance it adheres to the pattern of formal portraiture perfected by the great Fleming Anthony Van Dyck when he worked in Genoa at the beginning of the 1620's. Many excellent artists adopted this formula for their own use and it is not surprising that Philippe de Champaigne, a Fleming by birth, did so too. His portrait of Richelieu, however, is characterized by a cool and penetrating presentation of the Cardinal's incisive intelligence and indomitable will. The sweep of the voluminous silken robes, which trail behind the Cardinal into the space outside the picture at the right, suggest at once his worldly state and the uncompromising resolution and power that marked his eighteen effective years as Prime Minister of France. A shrewd statesman, Richelieu unified the land by force and liberated it from the threat of Spain, preaching always the "virtue of severity."

· 13 ·

JEAN TASSEL
(OR TASSET)
(ca. 1608–1667)

*Portrait of Catherine
de Montholon*

Oil on canvas, 21¼″ x 15¾″
Musée des Beaux Arts, Dijon

A modern critic in describing this picture has said that "it would be hard to find another portrait of this class in which the fine simplicity of the means employed harmonizes so perfectly with the austerity of the nun's vocation." The background as well as the white collar and the black cloth of her habit and headdress have been treated with a stark unrelieved geometrical simplicity and these flat neutral areas contrast sharply with the flesh tones and the modeling of the fanatically serious face and the beautiful slender and aristocratic hands. The use that is made of light and shadow is not dramatic or emotional, but is held within very narrow and subtle limits on the hands and at the sides of the face and at the corners of the stiff and spotless collar.

This elegant, if severe and forbidding, portrait belonged originally to the Ursuline Convent in Dijon, which was founded by Catherine de Montholon. Tassel probably painted it when he was working for the convent two years before the foundress' death in 1650. The Order of the Nuns of St. Ursula, which had been established in Italy a little more than a century before by St. Angela Merici of Brescia, had for its chief purpose the direction of "young maidens in the ways of the Lord." To judge from her portrait, the foundress of the convent in Dijon must have set a stern and disciplined standard for the young ladies whose education was entrusted to her.

· 14 ·

NICOLAS POUSSIN
(1594–1665)

The Rape of the Sabine Women

Oil on canvas, 60⅞″ x 82⅝″
Metropolitan Museum of Art,
New York. Purchase,
Harris B. Dick Fund, 1946.

In this picture and in one now in the Louvre that Poussin had painted several years before, around 1630, he treated a subject from Plutarch which had long been popular in Italian art. The story is about the founding of Rome by Romulus. There was a shortage of women in the new city and to remedy this lack Romulus, seen at the left standing high on a pedestal, had invited the Sabine tribe to a religious celebration. He is shown lifting a fold of his robe, which was a pre-arranged signal for each Roman to carry off a Sabine woman. Although according to the plan married women and their children were not to be molested, the foreground shows a little group of mother, babies, and an old nursemaid, protesting bitterly against their fate.

The strong verticals of the columns behind Romulus and of the pilasters of the building in the background form a static monumental contrast to the counterpoised diagonals of the violently active figures. The outthrust arms and legs of the overpowered women, their swaying draperies, their open mouths and shocked excited expressions strike loud notes exactly suited to the mood that the story demands and are good examples of Poussin's adaptation of his style to his subject matter. In preparing to paint his pictures of the rape of the Sabine women, Poussin made at least four drawings, which show how methodically he worked in order to evolve a satisfactory composition.

· 15 ·

NICOLAS POUSSIN
(1594–1665)

The Holy Family on the Steps
(ca. 1648)

Oil on canvas, 27⅛″ x 38⅜″
The National Gallery of Art,
Washington, D. C.
Samuel H. Kress Collection

It is generally agreed that this calm and monumental representation of the Holy Family sitting at the base of a flight of stairs was painted in the same year as the *Landscape with Diogenes,* 1648. Although the subject is Christian and not drawn from antique literature or philosophy, the little group of two women, a man, and two young children forming a pyramid in front of a mass of heavy Roman architecture, produce an effect of quiet controlled strength which can surely be called classical. The Virgin's very Roman head and the upper half of her body face the spectator directly, whereas the outstretched figure of St. Joseph, in shadow, is seen in pure profile. This firm shaping of the pyramid and the clear opposition of the architectural verticals with the horizontal lines of the steps produce an impression of weight and stability that is not static, but held in an equipoise that Poussin surely planned with great deliberation. He made a number of drawings in preparation for painting this picture.

· 16 ·

NICOLAS POUSSIN
(1594–1665)

Landscape with Diogenes
(1648)

Oil on canvas, 63″ x 87″
Louvre, Paris

Although this heroically beautiful landscape seems superbly self-sufficient, the two small but impressive figures in the right foreground tell us that it has a subject, a theme from classical Greece. The standing man is the cynical philosopher Diogenes, who one day saw a peasant drink from a pool aided only by his cupped hand. In an impulsive gesture of dedication, resolving to rely on Nature alone and to imitate the peasant, Diogenes threw away his own drinking cup. Poussin painted this picture for a banker from Genoa named Lumague, who lived in Paris and Lyons and was a friend of the powerful cardinals Richelieu and Mazarin. The painting belonged subsequently to the Duc de Richelieu and in 1665 went with the other pictures from his collection into that of Louis XIV.

In the *Landscape with Diogenes,* as in the two paintings devoted to the story of Phocion that he did in the same year, Poussin has endowed the landscape with an effect of noble strength and calm that suits admirably the character of the great philosopher Diogenes, who was so passionately devoted to nature. In the background at the left, glowing pale and high above the river that moves diagonally back into the depth of the picture, is a view of the buildings of the Vatican. A very similar view of the Vatican is the subject of a drawing by Poussin at Chantilly.

· 17 ·

NICOLAS POUSSIN
(1594–1665)

Self-Portrait

Oil on canvas, 38½" x 29¼"
Inscribed (in Latin): The
likeness of Nicolas Poussin,
painter from Les Andelys,
aged 56, in Rome in the
Jubilee Year of 1650.
Louvre, Paris

We know from Poussin's Italian contemporary, Dr. Giulio Mancini, that even in his first years in Rome, when he was still in his early thirties, Poussin had a noble appearance and way of dressing. In this self-portrait, painted when he was fifty-six, he has elected to show himself in his studio, wearing an impressively draped cloak, surely not ordinary everyday costume, but rather resembling academic dress. His chin is lifted proudly and the expression on his face is extremely sober, contributing, along with the rigid lines of the picture frames piled up against the wall behind him, to a general effect of severe dignity. Poussin is said to have had a preference for very simple frames. This severe picture contrasts strongly with another great self-portrait (now in Berlin) that he painted the year before, in which the facial expression, though thoughtful, is amiable, almost smiling. He himself regarded the Louvre's painting as the better of the two and a closer likeness. He painted it for his good friend in Paris, Paul Fréart de Chantelou, who had made a request for a portrait of Poussin three years before. Poussin had considered commissioning one of his contemporaries to paint him, but finally decided to do it himself, although it cost him a great effort, as he wrote to Chantelou, because he had not done a portrait for twenty-eight years. The painting in the background, showing a woman being embraced by a pair of hands, was interpreted by a seventeenth-century writer as symbolic of Painting and Friendship.

· 18 ·

PIERRE MIGNARD
(1612–1695)

*The Grand Dauphin
and his Family*
(1687)

Oil on canvas, 91⅜" x 119⅝"
Louvre, Paris

Maria Teresa, the Spanish Infanta who was married to Louis XIV in the famous ceremony on the Isle of Pheasants, bore him only one son, Louis the Grand Dauphin, whom we see here accompanied by his wife Marie Anne of Bavaria and their three sons, the king's grandchildren. The Grand Dauphin, heir to the throne of France, died in 1711, four years before his father Louis XIV. His eldest child, the Duke of Burgundy (1682-1712), who appears at the right of the picture as a little boy of five flourishing a lance, died (along with his wife and eldest child) the year after the Dauphin. It was the Duke of Burgundy's third son, born in 1710, the great-grandchild of Louis XIV, who succeeded his famous ancestor at his death in 1715 and came to the throne of France as Louis XV, "le Bien-Aimé," and reigned from 1715 until 1774. The other children of the Grand Dauphin shown in Mignard's family portrait are Charles of France, the Duke of Berry (1686-1714), beside his mother, and on the cushion in the center foreground, fondling a small black dog, Philippe of France, the Duke of Anjou (1683-1746), who became Philip V of Spain.

Family group portraits outdoors in open loggias or terraces with glimpses of trees and landscapes are not very usual in seventeenth-century France, but they were often painted around the middle of the century by Dutch artists such as Van der Helst, Mytens, and Barent Graet. The flying cupids at the upper right are probably reflections of Mignard's long years in Rome, where he was strongly influenced by the Carracci.

· 19 ·

HYACINTHE RIGAUD
(1659–1743)

Portrait of Louis XIV

Oil on canvas, 109⅞" x 74¾"
Signed and dated:
Hyacinthe Rigaud, 1701.
Louvre, Paris

When the king commissioned Rigaud to paint this portrait he intended to send it as a gift to King Philip V of Spain. Combining as it does, however, all the graces and charms of the king's person with the royal splendor of the whole kingdom of France, it pleased Louis so much that he ordered a copy made for the court at Madrid and kept this painting, Rigaud's dazzling original, to adorn the throne room at Versailles. The dark blue fabric of his ermine-lined robes of state, embroidered all over with the symbolic fleur-de-lis in gold, forms the upholstery of the great carved official chair behind the king and also covers the low hassock at the left, on which repose his crown and the Hand of Justice that once belonged to the Emperor Charles V. These objects, like the scepter so negligently and casually held by Louis and the massive jewel-studded sword of Charlemagne which he is wearing, are all part of the French royal treasure of St. Denis, preserved today in the Louvre.

Louis XIV was sixty-three when he posed for Rigaud, with fourteen years of his long and glorious reign still to run. The elegantly shaped legs, swathed in white silk, and neatly turned-out feet shod in rose and white, strike one of the classic poses of ballet, reminding us how this king loved to dance, how he performed in ballets himself, regarding dancing as "one of the most excellent and important disciplines for training the body," and how it was at Versailles that the conductor and composer Jean-Baptiste Lully flourished. La Fontaine, the author of the famous Fables, exclaimed about Louis XIV, "Do you think that the world has many kings of figure so beautiful, of appearance so fine? . . . when I see him I imagine I see Grandeur herself in person."

· 20 ·

NICOLAS DE
LARGILLIERE
(1656–1746)

Baroness de Prangins

Oil on canvas, 54⅜" x 41½"
Metropolitan Museum of Art,
New York. Purchase,
Rogers Fund, 1921.

The baroness, born Judith van Robais, came from a family of rich Flemish weavers and probably brought a considerable fortune to her marriage with Louis Guiguer, a banker and successful business man of Paris and London. He bought the barony of Prangins in 1723 and built on the shores of the Lake of Geneva a château that is still standing. This portrait of the baroness and that of her husband, which forms a pendant to it, were probably painted a few years before they acquired their titles, most likely in 1717 when they were in Paris at the time of a state visit by Peter the Great. Gossip has it that Peter was much taken with the baroness, and a caustic little French verse has come down to us which observes that the czar liked fat women and that he was attracted to our subject because she was so plump that it was difficult for her to get through doorways. In painting her portrait Largillière made no attempt to disguise her corpulence, but it must have bothered later owners of the picture, for at some time in the late eighteenth century, or the first half of the nineteenth, the outlines of her neck and cheeks were carefully retouched to give her a slimmer appearance. These repaints have now been removed and we see the baroness as she must have looked to the admiring eyes of Czar Peter the Great.

· 21 ·

BAUGIN
(active in the first half
of the seventeenth century)

*Still Life
with a Checkerboard*

Tempera and oil on wood,
21⅝″ x 28¾″
Louvre, Paris

In calling Baugin the greatest of the French still-life painters of the seventeenth century, Charles Sterling cites his almost musical instinct for plastic harmonies, his hushed refinement, and his extreme sobriety — all qualities marvelously represented in this rare still life, one of the three works definitely by this very rare painter. The same scholar points out that the numerous objects composing this assemblage are not brought together here by mere chance, but combine to form an allegory of the Five Senses. The crusty loaf of bread and the wine stand for Taste; the lute for Hearing; the flowers for Smelling; the mirror for Seeing; while the velvet purse, the playing cards, and the checkerboard represent Touching or Feeling. In the sixteenth century Cesare Ripa had established in his book on symbols the relation of a lute to allegorical representations of Hearing and of a bouquet to those of Smelling. The three peppermint carnations in the limpid crystal carafe are a direct tribute to Caravaggio, in whose work several closely similar vases are to be found. It is probably the geometrical severity of the black and white squares of the checkerboard, closed and fastened with gilt, that has reminded scholars of the work of the Spanish painters of still life, especially Zurbarán. The most striking aspect of the style of this picture is a peculiar clarity and sharpness of drawing, which isolates and defines each object in a quiet but independent assertion of its existence.

· 22 ·

**JEAN-BAPTISTE
MONNOYER**
(1636–1699)

Still Life

Oil on canvas, 44½″ x 49½″
Musée des Beaux Arts, Nancy

The opulence and richness of this great still life, which combines fruit and full-blown flowers with bas-relief, metalwork, and fringed and brocaded draperies, recalls the fact that Monnoyer, a native of Lille, studied painting in Antwerp, where he formed an early liking for sumptuous Flemish arrangements and acquired great skill in doing them. His paintings were extremely popular in France and it is easy to see from this still life how well his work would fit into the ambitious and elaborate decorative schemes that Le Brun planned and carried out for Louis XIV. Compared with the austerity of still lifes of the first half of the century, such as those by Baugin, or by a number of others who specialized in exquisite and chaste selections of objects, this billowing and luxurious composition is clearly in the taste of the "splendid century" and would have been able to hold its own in the heaviest and most overpowering architectural settings.

47

· 23 ·

CLAUDE LORRAIN
(CLAUDE GELLEE)
(1600–1682)

Sunrise
(ca. 1648)

Oil on canvas, 41¾″ x 53″
Metropolitan Museum of Art,
New York. Purchase,
Fletcher Fund, 1947

This painting of peasants, one on foot and two of them mounted, driving goats and cattle across the landscape and through a stream, has sometimes been thought to be a sunset rather than a sunrise scene. In the eighteenth century, however, when it was sold with other pictures from a French collection, it had a companion piece described in the catalogue as "Sunset, herdsmen driving home cattle across a river." This fact, along with the peculiar quality of the glow that gilds the figures and brightens the sky above and the distant landscape, provides a good reason for keeping the title of this painting "Sunrise."

In the book of two hundred drawings that Claude made after his own pictures as a record and a defense against the many artists who imitated him even during his lifetime, there is one that corresponds closely to this picture. On the back of it, in Claude's handwriting, is a notation that the painting itself was made for a patron in Lyons. Possibly this was the French patron named Parasson who lived in that city, as we know Claude made another picture for him, the *Flight into Egypt* now in the picture gallery at Dresden.

There are several drawings by Claude that he seems to have made in preparation for painting this picture, one of them a study for the herdsman driving the goats, which is in the Louvre, and another, in the Uffizi, showing the rosy cluster of buildings piled up on the hillside in the background.

· 24 ·

CLAUDE LORRAIN
(CLAUDE GELLEE)
(1600–1682)

*Landscape with
Sacrificial Procession*

Oil on canvas, 40″ x 50″
The Art Institute of Chicago

This picture and one in an English private collection that has for subject the classical story of Perseus were ordered by a papal chamberlain in Rome, the powerful patron of art, Cardinal Carlo Camillo Massimi, probably in 1672. Cardinal Massimi was an antiquarian and draughtsman, who was also Poussin's friend and patron. He was famous as a collector who had great learning and excellent taste. This picture and the Perseus were to form pendants to two others that Lorrain had painted for this same discriminating churchman some thirty years before.

A drawing for the *Landscape with Sacrificial Procession*, in the collection of the Queen at Windsor, bears an inscription in Claude's hand, describing it as representing the temple of Apollo at Delphi on Mount Parnassus, and informing us that in depicting this subject he followed the historian Justinus. Justinus's description is rather general, not specifying the shape of the temple, which Claude has made round. He did say, however, that it was situated "on a rock steep on all sides," and that there was "a deep fissure in the ground, which is open for oracles," a detail that Claude made very plain in the drawing, but showed less clearly in the finished painting.

Many years before he painted this picture, about the time of *Sunrise*, Claude had made another painting with a quite different composition, but also of a procession going to Delphi, for a rival Roman patron, Prince Camillo Pamphili. That picture still belongs to the Doria-Pamphili family.